Poet Eleven Vagabond Poet Ele

The Sweetness of Demons

14 Poems in Response to Baudelaire's Les Fleurs Du Mal

by Anne Pia

Vagabond Voices
Glasgow

First published on 29 March 2021 by
Vagabond Voices Publishing Ltd.,
Glasgow,
Scotland.

ISBN 978-1-913212-32-2

Printed and bound in Poland

Cover design by Mark Mechan

Typeset by Park Productions

The publisher acknowledges subsidy towards this publication from Creative Scotland

ALBA | CHRUTHACHAIL

For further information on Vagabond Voices, see the website,
www.vagabondvoices.co.uk

Contents

Introduction

His work is "an iceberg...certain stars in our galaxy
are so faint that none of our instruments can detect
them, yet their presence can be inferred from the
way in which their gravity tugs on the invisible stars"
(Claude Pichois; 1996)

Charles Baudelaire was born in Paris in 1821 and apart from
a trip to Mauritius and Calcutta in his twenties which his
stepfather arranged to distract him from his dissolute lifestyle,
Baudelaire spent most of his life there. He died in 1867 in a
hospital near l'Étoile in Paris cared for by his mother whom
he adored.

Baudelaire wrote extensively. He was a translator of Edgar
Allan Poe, was heralded as a pioneering art and music critic,
and known for his political outspokenness and activism; he
took part in the Revolutions of 1848 and wrote for a revo-
lutionary newspaper. His contribution to European artistic
development has been both significant and magnificent.
However, it is for his poetry that he is most admired... poetry
that has inspired, delighted, challenged and shocked read-
ers for generations, bringing new and exciting dimensions
and a stark realism to the poetic output of his predecessors.
Baudelaire broke with poetic tradition, an innovative stylist
who exposed in literature "a realm which had until then been
unexplored... hell, anguish, tedium, isolation and despair...

not evil but sin; man's frailty and repentance."[1] De Gourmont in 1905 wrote admiringly of what he called Baudelaire's "intense humanity" in his attitude to the reality of existence and his unwillingness to be "corrupted by sentimentalism". Baudelaire uncovered the unbeautiful, the shameful and the ugly. He has been called the father of Impressionism, the founder of Modernism – the "urban modernity" of his output distinguishing him from his European Romantic counterparts – and described as "restoring poetry to its true destiny" (Raynaud 1917). Throughout his work, the voices of literary giants of Western civilisation reverberate still. Baudelaire takes his place alongside them and is arguably one of the greatest poets that ever lived.

Les Fleurs du Mal, his best-known work, was first published in June 1857 causing outrage in the press and subsequent disciplinary action by the French authorities for the scandalous nature of some of the content. Following a judicial process both writer and publishing house were fined. The collection was published a second time in 1861 with the exclusion of six poems. These were ultimately included years later and now form part of the work as we know it.

A Poet's Choice

I have been wanting to revisit Baudelaire's *Les Fleurs du Mal* for some time. The collection is a vivid and often stark representation of a society in the midst of change: the industrial revolution accompanied by a period of heightened Romanticism and idealism in counterpoint. The poems are as relevant and fresh for today's world struggling with dwindling

---

1   Richardson 1994

natural resources, an era of pandemics, the continual need to adapt to technological change, and a dewy-eyed liberalism – a faltering remnant of the sixties and seventies, as right-wing politics gather strength.

There are resonances for me too in personal and political preoccupations; his passion is as timeless as human nature and as everlasting as the human spirit: seeking, soaring or despairing. In Baudelaire's acid and beguiling poetry, frailty, despair and joy are all present. He luxuriates and furiously dismisses. He rages and yet he speaks soft words. He is tender. He yearns, aches and seductively persuades. A creator of vivid visuals and sublimely evocative music, a conjuror of mist, soft light and of exotic scents, a sculptor and a weaver of tapestry and texture through a mere interplay of words and skilful verse and stanza, Baudelaire – whether jubilant or bitter – is never light-hearted, always honest, intense, disturbing. In their correspondence Sainte Beuve wrote "sadness... is what will be most esteemed in you." Angry and despairing at his mother's remarriage in 1828 after his father's death in 1827 and his own perceived loss of her, he wrote "I belong only to you." It is that emotion, that disillusionment and yearning melancholy that drives his poetry. It is that seeking of the impossible and the unfindable – the searing pain of it – that is so compelling even today. As Mauriac wrote, he was "both the knife and the wound".

If loving easily, often and in diverse ways indicates a love of life, Baudelaire's appetite for all that the universe... experienced through emotion and lived and breathed in the blood... is supreme, palpable, affecting and alarmingly infectious. Alive to all that surrounds him, he assails what is basic and raw in his readers. He enjoyed women and revelled in them. He was wholehearted and dogged in pursuit. While his liaisons differed widely, the women he wrote about

– prostitutes, actresses, women of chance encounters, women of society and women of French salons, elegant lunches and culture – all emerge as supremely glorious. These women are beautiful and dignified without and within, alluring to the touch, eye and ear and inviting as they move; women to be cherished, to be revered as well as savoured.

In his poem "A Une Passante", the connection and desire between him and a complete stranger is as powerful as in the many poems to his long-term lover Jeanne Duval, his "Vénus Noire". In "Le Léthe", one of many poems for Duval, his heady immersion in the black waters of the underworld is as compulsive, lust-laden, turbulent and damming as their lovemaking. "L'Invitation au Voyage", possibly his best-known poem and written to his short-term lover, the actress Marie Daubrun, is unfailingly persuasive in its understatement and suggestiveness. Measured and full of sexual ambiguity, it is richly evocative of a Vermeer painting, and yet as enticing as a Mozart andante with its form and structure straining to maintain decency and respectability. "L' Harmonie di Soir", "Le Flacon" and "Que diras-tu ce Soir?", the poems to his muse and spiritual love Apollonie Sabatier, evoke Dante's Beatrice. They are melancholic in their longing and at the same time prudish, reverential and reflective. In a short letter to this distant beauty he writes "les sentiments profonds ont une pudeur qui ne veut pas être violée" ("some feelings are so deep that their purity remains absolute").

His love poems capture too the uniqueness of his relationships. Within them he is as different a lover as his beloved, distilling in diverse poetic forms the character and temperament of each. At the same time there remains a solid consistency in his profound regard and respect for every one of them, irrespective of age, social position, ethnicity or colour. Some would argue that *la femme* is what matters to a lust-driven, needy man, but I am more inclined to the view held by others that Baudelaire was a man of the highest morality who, as Jackson wrote in 2005, "subverts the conventional in order to reveal the hypocrisy of society of that time".

In truth, Baudelaire's women are modern women… powerful, free, sexually active, often dominant; with their own sexual appetites, they are fluid, open and undoubtedly his equals. These are self-directed women who have made choices and "evolved" (Simone De Beauvoir's assertion) – women who have "become women" through the lives they have decided to lead. They are in my view, indisputably women of today.

Baudelaire championed the dispossessed, the suffering and the disadvantaged: "Caïn et Abel" and "Bohémiens en Voyage" for instance. Having himself rejected the benefits of social advantage, he was more at home with society's underclass, its waste and individuals wasted through industrialisation. He raged at judgemental attitudes as in for example, "Delphine et Hippolyte" with clear references to Dante's Inferno and parodied the excesses of self-righteous moralism. He confronted xenophobia and racism. He refuted what is self-congratulatory and lofty. Like many artists of his time, through poetry he delved into the occult – "the secret harmony of things" as Hazareesingh writes in 2015; at times he leads us on fear-inducing, Virgilian/Dantesque journeys through the sewers and the underworld. His is a God-damming, mocking theology but nonetheless one of hope, possibility, happiness and light bliss glimpsed but cruelly and constantly elusive.

Throughout my life my relationship with France has been precious. Its literature and artistic output, its culture in galleries, cathedrals, bookshops, cafés and the kind of shops you might find in Le Marais or L'Ile Saint-Louis, loved as my own. For me then, Baudelaire was an obvious source of inspiration. He captures the essential qualities of the French language, for, read or spoken, it is elegant and contained, abstract and ethereal, precise in word and evocative in sound and texture. Like a Bach fugue, it has a quintessential clarity. He is unmistakably and for me irresistibly French: rational, reflective, introspective and philosophical – a forerunner of some key thinkers of our own time… Baudrillard's writing on symbolism and Foucault's ontological stance on sexuality and power structures within societal frameworks and contexts. Most of all however, I believe that his internationalism carries an important message especially for today. His wider vision and engagement with cultures and traditions beyond his own are the source of his genius. While he wrote at a certain time and from a certain place, the uniquely fertile, truthful and universal nature of his writing is founded on his interaction and continual dialogue with the work of writers and thinkers who went before him, as well as the intellectuals of his day, and on a creativity that works within a dimension that goes beyond France and indeed Europe. And yet it is also solidly grounded in the realism of his day.

It is for all of these reasons that I have returned to this poet of poets. But more specifically, I have wanted to explore the vocabulary and structures of a language other than my own and immerse myself in another form of expression, a language not of my time nor of the writing that currently surrounds me. I have chosen a language for my poetry which I felt best represents the mood, atmosphere and sound of the original French. Through my writing I have wanted to enjoy a much wider cultural and linguistic experience and the effect of its "gravity"[2] on my own writing and my intimate musings.

---

2   Pichois 1996

The fourteen poems in this collection are a response to those poems in *Les Fleurs du Mal* which compelled and inspired me most – poems I was least able to resist. They have been chosen for no other reason than that I could not let the them rest quietly on the pages where I found them. They commanded my attention, took root and something flourished. I have arranged them so that each of my own poems sits alongside the French it originated from, together with my translation. It is possible to present Baudelaire's poetry in a language other than French. It is however, an almost impossible task to translate the richness, sumptuousness and raw reality of images, the transient effect of light and colour, which assault, dazzle and tease… evocations captured in sound, absorbed through the skin. Baudelaire "eludes translation" as Lloyd (2005) boldly states. My tentative representations, interpretations, I hope, give at least some faint sense of his art. In translating I simply wanted to render the French, to excavate his words and try to find the best pairing in English. And in creating my own poems… my responses, my way of working was to read and reread the French, allowing each poem to settle in my mind and then to take on the voice of seducer, seduced or both. Some of my poems are a fantasy. For I found in Baudelaire, a means somehow of exploring my own sexual boundaries, darknesses and secret imaginings… and if we're honest, lives or experiences I and many of us might have lived but didn't dare.

The Sweetness of Demons

Le Revenant

Comme les anges á l'oeil fauve,
Je reviendrai dans ton alcôve
Et vers toi glisserai sans bruit
Avec les ombres de la nuit;
Et je te donnerai, ma brune,
Des baisers froids comme la lune
Et des caresses de serpent
Autour d'une fosse rampant.
Quand viendra le matin livide,
Tu trouveras ma place vide,
Où jusqu'au soir il fera froid.
Comme d'autres par la tendresse
Sur ta vie et sur ta jeunesse,
Moi, je veux régner par l'effroi.

The Revenant

Like lust driven angels / I will return to your lair / as silently as the shades of night, / I will glide towards you. / And, my dark beauty, / my kisses will be as chill as the moon; / like a snake coiling / upwards from the grave, / I will enfold you. / When pale morning comes. /

Sweet the Chill

The chill of brocade and satin, my lush coverings,
is sweet with the cold ash and scent of you
the rot of pit and broken slab that mark
the home we chose for you;
your world and not yet mine.
A new nocturnal coupling for us
your whisper-like covering of me;
gossamer teasing solid bone and gristle
you slip whole into my space
a noiseless breaching
by the light of a cold moon;
your scattered kisses sting
like driving snow;
and like a snake uncoiled
your glacial tongue, a savage piercing
turns my melting to ice
and I am your willing prey.
Then when you, my unholy prize,
slide away into early daylight
I your fearful, dark beauty,
am pregnant with your presence,
quick with our untellable fable.

*there will be nothing / but empty space beside you and a chill air / that
lingers into evening. / Others rule with tenderness. / Over your life
and your youth / I will hold sway through fear.*

3

À Une Passante

La rue assourdissante autour de moi hurlait.
Longue, mince, en grand deuil, douleur majestueuse,
Une femme passa, d'une main fastueuse
Soulevant, balançant le feston et l'ourlet;

Agile et noble, avec sa jambe de statue.
Moi, je buvais, crispé comme un extravagant,
Dans son oeil, ciel livide où germe l'ouragan,
La douceur qui fascine et le plaisir qui tue.

Un éclair... puis la nuit! — Fugitive beauté
Dont le regard m'a fait soudainement renaître,
Ne te verrai-je plus que dans l'éternité?

Ailleurs, bien loin d'ici! trop tard! jamais peut-être!
Car j'ignore où tu fuis, tu ne sais où je vais,
Ô toi que j'eusse aimée, ô toi qui le savais!

To A Woman Passing By

*All around me the street's roar was deafening. / A tall, slender
woman passed by in full funeral attire. / Majestic in mourning, her
movements deft and stately, / she adjusted the hem of her skirts and
her veils. // And I caught a glimpse of her regal hand, a shapely leg. /
Aroused and overcome with desire, / I drank in the hurricane lurking
in the paleness of her eyes, / her tenderness and the irresistible promise
of destruction and sweet pleasure. // Then in a lightening flash...
dark night fell around me! Oh fleeting beauty, / I was reborn at the
look you gave me. / Will I see you again or only in Eternity perhaps?
// Somewhere far from here? Too late, too late! Maybe never. / I don't
know where you are rushing to and you cannot know where I am
going. / Oh how I would have loved you! And you, who knew it well.*

Imaginings

Such an unforgettable hurricane lurking in your eyes madame
as you stripped away my skin, like bark off a tree
and laid bare trembling sapwood.

At the hem of imagined petticoats
I fêted you with flowers
laid garlands
at the proud bloom of your warm breasts
curved and contained by a simple costume.
Like the soft silhouette of a strung harp
 I traced the sweep of your back
and the sculpted spareness of your shoulders;
sated with the salt mines at the parting of your thighs
I fed you the juices of ripe pomegranates
and sweet wine from deep earthenware jugs;
for you my love, I spread rich satins
to welcome your unscarfed head
and soothe your sighing,
I placed rugs from Isfahan at your feet
and linens to cool and still your restive palms;
at your bidding, I bathed you whole in silken sheets
wove willow baskets for you to rest in.

But what a short dwelling was ours,
magnificent and ornamental in black lace
you took your sudden, silent leave,
and in parting,
the possibility of chance discovery
left to the wiles of day-to-day
and tempests
to illusion and eternity.

Les Bohémiens en Voyage

La tribu prophétique aux prunelles ardentes
Hier s'est mise en route, emportant ses petits
Sur son dos, ou livrant à leurs fiers appétits
Le trésor toujours prêt des mamelles pendantes.

Les hommes vont à pied sous leurs armes luisantes
Le long des chariots où les leurs sont blottis,
Promenant sur le ciel des yeux appesantis
Par le morne regret des chimères absentes.

Du fond de son réduit sablonneux, le grillon,
Les regardant passer, redouble sa chanson;
Cybèle, qui les aime, augmente ses verdures,

Fait couler le rocher et fleurir le désert
Devant ces voyageurs, pour lesquels est ouvert
L'empire familier des ténèbres futures.

Secure the Gates

1

Then suddenly they came, shadowing the walls of the Old
    City
like hired assassins or a scene from an opera,
our louche guides to liberation
or to an exorcism of the mind rather,
perverted
by the Herodian darkness
of thresholds painted
with the frail, fresh blood of innocents,
and to deliverance from our nightmares,
sisters and mothers run through and
left stiffening on the cold stakes of Kalashnikovs;
and as the strobe lighting of bombardment created fiendish
    slideshows
of body parts and decomposition,
of builders blocks on industrial wasteland, once a treasured
    citadel,
of the hollowed-out caves of El Nahasin it's bathing wells
    now parched
where East and West, made mankind's history,
against the satanic counterpoint
of shells and bullets, a Paganini[1] concerto perhaps,
heads down, we tenderly gathered our sleeping babes
new hatched chicks still in their shell,
in stealth herded our gentle grandmothers,
loaded dull-eyed fathers
onto whatever with wheels
and promised blessed manna.

---

1   Paganini was reputed to have made a pact with the Devil.

Travellers on the Road

The tribe of prophets, eyes aflame, / Set off yesterday, carrying their children / On their backs, or leaving them to proudly enjoy / The ever-present treasures of a mother's drooping breast. // The men walk, heavy in their gleaming weaponry / Skirt the wagons carrying their kinsfolk who huddle together / And who scan the skies, eyes heavy / With despair at vanquished ghosts. // From the depths of his nest, watching them pass by / The cricket sings all the more loudly, / Cybele who loves them, blooms ever more abundantly, // Before the eyes of a displaced people / She turns rocks to rivers and deserts to beds of wild flowers / For them, that familiar empire of darkness opens up.

We left water taps rusted with stories of ancestors,
stone circles ringed with our bonds,
pots aged with laughter and what it is to be home,
while our children watched a fantasy undreamt of.
In files dumb with fear and weeping
we followed hope, salvation and these unkent disciples
    towards
a star filled desert and
a new Messiah.

2

May your children sleep well in safe beds
oh brothers and sisters of the West,
while kindly fairies shape their dreams
the witches of our young lie in the filth of your borders
famine at your gates,
and cold on rough mats for sleeping
they feast on the spells of men
and vampires inhabit the spirits of despots and soldiers;
the rich man's table is closely guarded, his own secure;
Babel's offspring, the science of many continents
has built your tower and your bridges for travellers,
but who now will nourish your people
in its cleansed incarceration?

Femmes Damnées: Delphine et Hippolyte

À la pâle clarté des lampes languissantes,
Sur de profonds coussins tout imprégnés d'odeur,
Hippolyte rêvait aux caresses puissantes
Qui levaient le rideau de sa jeune candeur.
Elle cherchait, d'un oeil troublé par la tempête,
De sa naïveté le ciel déjà lointain,
Ainsi qu'un voyageur qui retourne la tête
Vers les horizons bleus dépassés le matin.
De ses yeux amortis les paresseuses larmes,
L'air brisé, la stupeur, la morne volupté,
Ses bras vaincus, jetés comme de vaines armes,
Tout servait, tout parait sa fragile beauté.
Étendue à ses pieds, calme et pleine de joie,
Delphine la couvait avec des yeux ardents,
Comme un animal fort qui surveille une proie,
Après l'avoir d'abord marquée avec les dents.
Beauté forte à genoux devant la beauté frêle,
Superbe, elle humait voluptueusement
Le vin de son triomphe, et s'allongeait vers elle,
Comme pour recueillir un doux remercîment.
Elle cherchait dans l'oeil de sa pâle victime
Le cantique muet que chante le plaisir,
Et cette gratitude infinie et sublime
Qui sort de la paupière ainsi qu'un long soupir.
- "Hippolyte, cher coeur, que dis-tu de ces choses?
Comprends-tu maintenant qu'il ne faut pas offrir
L'holocauste sacré de tes premières roses
Aux souffles violents qui pourraient les flétrir?
Mes baisers sont légers comme ces éphémères
Qui caressent le soir les grands lacs transparents,
Et ceux de ton amant creuseront leurs ornières

Precious... Unblessed...Forever Unnamed

Look now Hippolyte,
my uncertain lover, flushed pale,
see the watchful moon, our sole confidante,
when deep within these earthen walls
finally unseen,
my kisses, no longer captive,
settled lightly...a storm of fireflies...
on your great warrior frame,
feathering the ebb and flow, the ready summits of you;
like melting caramel, though timid at first
you softened at my touch
and within your bower's full blossoming, in the end bidden,
I savoured sweet damsons and the tang of nutmeg
which call me back
for our spray and scatter made oceans of our bedchamber.
And now, great queen, like those enemy tribes before you,
you lie at my side, my beauty,
felled and unruly,
and on pillows heavy with the scented rainfall of a first
    spring,
your gaze is on vanquished girlhood.

A still, soundless air surrounds you my Delphine,
I am caught in the evenness of your breath
I spin in your breathlessness
in closeness we are wordless
and as you watch me from where you lie resting
before your silent solidity I am both empty space,
and a fig tree, ever fruiting,
it's yield always ripe.

Comme des chariots ou des socs déchirants;
Ils passeront sur toi comme un lourd attelage
De chevaux et de boeufs aux sabots sans pitié...
Hippolyte, ô ma soeur! tourne donc ton visage,
Toi, mon âme et mon coeur, mon tout et ma moitié,
Tourne vers moi tes yeux pleins d'azur et d'étoiles!
Pour un de ces regards charmants, baume divin,
Des plaisirs plus obscurs je lèverai les voiles
Et je t'endormirai dans un rêve sans fin!"
Mais Hippolyte alors, levant sa jeune tête:
- "Je ne suis point ingrate et ne me repens pas,
Ma Delphine, je souffre et je suis inquiète,
Comme après un nocturne et terrible repas.
Je sens fondre sur moi de lourdes épouvantes
Et de noirs bataillons de fantômes épars,
Qui veulent me conduire en des routes mouvantes
Qu'un horizon sanglant ferme de toutes parts.
Avons-nous donc commis une action étrange?
Explique, si tu peux, mon trouble et mon effroi:
Je frissonne de peur quand tu me dis: 'Mon ange!'
Et cependant je sens ma bouche aller vers toi.
Ne me regarde pas ainsi, toi, ma pensée!
Toi que j'aime à jamais, ma soeur d'élection,
Quand même tu serais une embûche dressée
Et le commencement de ma perdition!"
Delphine secouant sa crinière tragique,
Et comme trépignant sur le trépied de fer,
L'oeil fatal, répondit d'une voix despotique:
- "Qui donc devant l'amour ose parler d'enfer?
"Maudit soit à jamais le rêveur inutile
Qui voulut le premier, dans sa stupidité,
S'éprenant d'un problème insoluble et stérile,
Aux choses de l'amour mêler l'honnêteté!

I am your angel, craving a slave's unholy capture
your wakeful warrior, seeking no other conquest but you.
We have drawn back the drapes on innocence
my first full roses of discovery have bloomed for you alone
and in this chamber together we are abundant and
    victorious
but the cruel eye of the moon you speak of is upon me
stark and unblinking in the dreadful black of this night.
I fear for us and my reckless, insatiable loving of you.
In the coming of daylight
only a half, unsmiling light,
our shared delight one in the other,
precious,
unblessed
and forever unnamed.

Women Damned: Delphine et Hippolyte

In the pale dying light of flickering lamps, / On odour-steeped, deep cushions, / Hippolyte pondered the power of tenderness, / caresses that had lifted the curtain from her youthful innocence. // As a traveller troubled by the storm / looking back, she sought / the now faraway skies of her unknowing / and the past pure blue horizons of morning. // Her slow falling tears from unseeing eyes, / the shattered air, her numbness, the dark delight, / her vanquished arms scattered like worthless weapons / all enhanced and all proclaimed her fragile beauty. // Stretched out at her feet, calm and joyful, / Delphine, eyes aflame, gazed in wonder at her, / Like a strong animal watching its prey, / having already marked it with its teeth. // Strong beauty kneeling before frail beauty, / proudly, she voluptuously inhaled the bouquet / of her triumph, and lay down beside her / As if to gather to herself some gentle appreciation. // She sought to find in the eyes of her wan victim, / a silent hymn of unguarded pleasure / and eternal, sublime gratitude / that drops from the eyelids like a never-ending sigh. // 'Hippolyte, my darling, what say you to these things? / Do

Celui qui veut unir dans un accord mystique
L'ombre avec la chaleur, la nuit avec le jour,
Ne chauffera jamais son corps paralytique
À ce rouge soleil que l'on nomme l'amour!
Va, si tu veux, chercher un fiancé stupide;
Cours offrir un coeur vierge à ses cruels baisers;
Et, pleine de remords et d'horreur, et livide,
Tu me rapporteras tes seins stigmatisés...
On ne peut ici-bas contenter qu'un seul maître!"
Mais l'enfant, épanchant une immense douleur,
Cria soudain: "Je sens s'élargir dans mon être
Un abîme béant; cet abîme est mon coeur!
Brûlant comme un volcan, profond comme le vide!
Rien ne rassasiera ce monstre gémissant
Et ne rafraîchira la soif de l'Euménide
Qui, la torche à la main, le brûle jusqu'au sang.
Que nos rideaux fermés nous séparent du monde,
Et que la lassitude amène le repos!
Je veux m'anéantir dans ta gorge profonde
Et trouver sur ton sein la fraîcheur des tombeaux!"
- Descendez, descendez, lamentables victimes,
Descendez le chemin de l'enfer éternel!
Plongez au plus profond du gouffre, où tous les crimes,
Flagellés par un vent qui ne vient pas du ciel,
Bouillonnent pêle-mêle avec un bruit d'orage.
Ombres folles, courez au but de vos désirs;
Jamais vous ne pourrez assouvir votre rage,
Et votre châtiment naîtra de vos plaisirs.
Jamais un rayon frais n'éclaira vos cavernes;
Par les fentes des murs des miasmes fiévreux
Filtrent en s'enflammant ainsi que des lanternes
Et pénètrent vos corps de leurs parfums affreux.
L'âpre stérilité de votre jouissance

you now / understand that you must not surrender / the blessed immolation of your first roses / to violent gusts which may wither them as they bloom? // My kisses are as delicate as mayflies / alighting gently at nightfall on wide expanses of clear water, / And those of a man will scar your flesh / Like chariot wheels or the blade of a plough ripping up your flesh; // Like a heavy cavalcade of horses and oxen, / they will run you over with unrelenting hooves / Hippolyte, my sister, turn your face towards me, / You are my soul and my heart, my all and the other half of who I am. // Turn those eyes full of the azure and stars of the sky towards me, / for a beguiling look from you, balm of the gods, / I would reveal the darkest of delights / And soothe you to sleep, to dream forever.' // But Hippolyte then, raising her young head: / 'I am not at all ungrateful and repent nothing, / my Delphine, I am suffering and troubled / as if after a terrible night of gluttony. // I feel the weight of heavy fear collapsing upon me/ and legions of black phantoms circling / trying to lead me on distant unending journeys / barred at every crossroad by bloodied horizons. // Have we then, done something out of the ordinary? / If you can, explain the reasons for my disquiet and terror: / I tremble with fear when you call me "My angel" / Yet, I feel my mouth moving towards yours. // Do not look at me like that my silk-soft flower / You whom I love eternally, my chosen sister, / and yet you are a snare set to entrap me / and the source of my damnation.' // Delphine shaking her head in tragic pose / and as if tapping her feet repeatedly on unyielding iron / shot her a deathly look and replied in a commanding voice: / 'Who dares speak of Hell in the face of love? // Damn him forever, whoever he is, that useless philosopher / who in his ignorance, desperate to be the first, / tackles in vain, the intractable problem / of how to mix honesty with matters of love. // He, who through some other worldly pact / attempts to unite shade and warmth, night with day, / will never warm his petrified body / in the heat of the red-hot sun of lovemaking! // Go if you will, seek your blundering betrothed; / Run, offer your virgin heart to his stinging kisses / Then full of remorse and horror, drained of colour, / You will return your breasts pierced with his imprint. // Here on this earth, we can but please one master!' // But the young girl, unable to contain such immense pain / Cried out suddenly 'I feel a great abyss opening throughout my being; / this gaping abyss is my heart // Burning like a volcano, as deep as the void! / Nothing will appease this groaning monster nor

Altère votre soif et roidit votre peau,
Et le vent furibond de la concupiscence
Fait claquer votre chair ainsi qu'un vieux drapeau.
Loin des peuples vivants, errantes, condamnées,
À travers les déserts courez comme les loups;
Faites votre destin, âmes désordonnées,
Et fuyez l'infini que vous portez en vous!

slake the thirst of the Eumenides, / who torch in hand, will burn my very blood. // Oh let us leave our drapes closed, and cut off from the world / may lassitude bring us rest! / I will seek my destruction within the depths of your throat / and on your breast, find the freshness of a tombstone.' // -Down, down, go down you sorry victims / on the road to eternal damnation! / Dive to the bottom of the deep, where all crimes / whipped up by a wind which comes not from the sky // Broil and bubble and bang together like thunder claps. / Demented souls, fly towards your folly and the object of your desires; / Never will you tame your lust / And your pleasures will ever seed your punishment. // Never will a sunbeam light up your dungeon, / From cracks in the rock feverish vapours will flare like lanterns / And consume your flesh with their terrible stench. // The bitter sterility of your joy / Will warp your thirst and stiffen your skin / and the infernal whirlwind of bestial desire 2 / Will split open your flesh like an ancient flailing flag. // Far from the living, the wanderers and the damned, / Across deserts, run like the wolf; / Fashion your fate, oh unnatural souls, / and take flight from the unyielding infinity / that resides without end within you.

---

2   A reference to *The Divine Comedy*, "la bufera infernal" in Canto V of Dante's *Inferno* is the whirlwind that tossed the adulterous lovers Paolo and Francesca around for eternity. The adulterous kiss "la bocca mi baciò tutto tremante".

Le Léthé

Viens sur mon coeur, âme cruelle et sourde,
Tigre adoré, monstre aux airs indolents;
Je veux longtemps plonger mes doigts tremblants
Dans l'épaisseur de ta crinière lourde;

Dans tes jupons remplis de ton parfum
Ensevelir ma tête endolorie,
Et respirer, comme une fleur flétrie,
Le doux relent de mon amour défunt.

Je veux dormir! dormir plutôt que vivre!
Dans un sommeil aussi doux que la mort,
J'étalerai mes baisers sans remords
Sur ton beau corps poli comme le cuivre.

Pour engloutir mes sanglots apaisés
Rien ne me vaut l'abîme de ta couche;
L'oubli puissant habite sur ta bouche,
Et le Léthé coule dans tes baisers.

À mon destin, désormais mon délice,
J'obéirai comme un prédestiné;
Martyr docile, innocent condamné,
Dont la ferveur attise le supplice,

Je sucerai, pour noyer ma rancoeur,
Le népenthès et la bonne ciguë
Aux bouts charmants de cette gorge aiguë
Qui n'a jamais emprisonné de coeur.

Black Venus

Unassailable woman
let us not speak of love or gentle things
but together instead let us seek the blackened soil
of infected wasteland
and bathe in rivers of honey and over-sweet tar;
like a stray nightingale
let me nest in the labyrinth of your skirts
and carousing in cocoa and cloves
on the down of your breasts
my eager lips will lullaby;
oh turn your head towards me
and offer license to my trembling fingers
make flames of your eyes to make swift my passage
to sweet self-immolation;
in the half light of evening summon the hallowed shadows
that will consume me;
like Salome place each of your transgressions on a silver platter,
spice my raw red wine with your thirsting,
make sweetmeats of your demons,
and I will gladly feast on them and grow fat;
Charon awaits us, his oars prime for the crossing
come, let us loosen the ties
and laughing, surrender.

The Lethe

*Oh cruel, deaf soul, come and rest here on my heart. / Adored tigress,
insouciant monster, / I want to plunge my trembling fingers / deep into
your luxurious, mass of hair; // Forever bury my tortured head / in
your skirts full of the scent of you, / and like a wilted flower, / inhale
the sweetness of a love which is no more. // I want to sleep! To sleep*

rather than to live! / In that oblivion as sweet as death, / I will scatter
relentless kisses / on the burnished copper of your beautiful skin. //
Only the deep abyss of your bed / can contain and quieten my sobbing;
/ powerful obliteration lives on your lips / and the Lethe drops in a
steady flow from your kisses. // Like a man doomed, I will obey fate,
henceforth my delight. / I am a willing martyr, an innocent condemned,
/ whose agony is intensified by ardour. // To drown my rancour, / I will
suck hemlock and nepenthe / from the buds of your charming breasts. /
They have never enclosed a beating heart.

Le Balcon

Mère des souvenirs, maîtresse des maîtresses,
Ô toi, tous mes plaisirs! ô toi, tous mes devoirs!
Tu te rappelleras la beauté des caresses,
La douceur du foyer et le charme des soirs,
Mère des souvenirs, maîtresse des maîtresses!

Les soirs illuminés par l'ardeur du charbon,
Et les soirs au balcon, voilés de vapeurs roses.
Que ton sein m'était doux! que ton coeur m'était bon!
Nous avons dit souvent d'impérissables choses
Les soirs illuminés par l'ardeur du charbon.

Que les soleils sont beaux dans les chaudes soirées!
Que l'espace est profond! que le coeur est puissant!
En me penchant vers toi, reine des adorées,
Je croyais respirer le parfum de ton sang.
Que les soleils sont beaux dans les chaudes soirées!

La nuit s'épaississait ainsi qu'une cloison,
Et mes yeux dans le noir devinaient tes prunelles,
Et je buvais ton souffle, ô douceur! ô poison!
Et tes pieds s'endormaient dans mes mains fraternelles.
La nuit s'épaississait ainsi qu'une cloison.

Je sais l'art d'évoquer les minutes heureuses,
Et revis mon passé blotti dans tes genoux.
Car à quoi bon chercher tes beautés langoureuses
Ailleurs qu'en ton cher corps et qu'en ton coeur si doux?
Je sais l'art d'évoquer les minutes heureuses!

Ces serments, ces parfums, ces baisers infinis,

Never Bid Me Farewell

Bring me rivulets of silver and
unlaced, in silken bands and airborne ribbons
let me dance;
I am a humming bird
a-quiver in columbine
caught in the sweet syrup of honeysuckle.
My extravagant lover
on the soft shoreline of my back
lay down grateful wreaths to love
and with rough kisses salt my open skin;
like mellow fruits, consume each of my lips
and swallow nothing other than my breath
warm words and woodsmoke;
carpet my bedchamber with golden grasses
where amidst love's still-warm residue
I might seek rest;
look no further than a balcony
the dark trace of cheeks and brow
the welcome crypt of hair tangle
the tease of warm velvet,
never-ending tide pools
the ever-sweet familiarity of haste.

The Balcony

*Mother of memories, mistress of all mistresses, / You are the source
of all my pleasure and object of all my devotion. / Remember the
beauty of our caressing, the gentle delights of hearth and home, / our
evenings spent there together. / Mother of memories, mistress of all
mistresses. // The ardent blaze and heat of those coal-lit evenings,
/ those long evenings on the balcony, bathed in the pink glow of a
setting sun, you and I. / How soft your breasts were! How I savoured*

Renaîtront-ils d'un gouffre interdit à nos sondes,
Comme montent au ciel les soleils rajeunis
Après s'être lavés au fond des mers profondes?
— Ô serments! ô parfums! ô baisers infinis!

the goodness in your heart. / We spoke words that will never die. / The ardent blaze and heat of those coal-lit evenings. // How glorious are the suns in the heat of evening. / How deep space is! How mighty the heart! / As I bent over you, adored queen of women, / I inhaled it seemed, the very scent of your blood. / How glorious are the suns in the heat of evening. // Night's thick walls gathered us in / and in the black of night my eyes found yours. / I swallowed your breath. Oh sweet poison! / Your stilled feet slumbered deep in my brotherly hands. / Night's thick walls gathered us in. // How well I know the art of reliving moments of happiness / And I relive the oblivion of being between your knees. / Where else should I seek your languid charms / if not from within your cherished body and gentle heart / How well I know the art of reliving moments of happiness. // Our vows, these scents, kisses without end, / can we bring them back them from the abyss where they lie beyond our reach, / and like fresh suns washed by the deep, / rise high from the sea bed once more. / Oh vows. Oh such perfume. Oh kisses without end.

À Une Malabaraise

Tes pieds sont aussi fins que tes mains, et ta hanche
Est large à faire envie à la plus belle blanche;
À l'artiste pensif ton corps est doux et cher;
Tes grands yeux de velours sont plus noirs que ta chair.
Aux pays chauds et bleus où ton Dieu t'a fait naître,
Ta tâche est d'allumer la pipe de ton maître,
De pourvoir les flacons d'eaux fraîches et d'odeurs,
De chasser loin du lit les moustiques rôdeurs,
Et, dès que le matin fait chanter les platanes,
D'acheter au bazar ananas et bananes.
Tout le jour, où tu veux, tu mènes tes pieds nus,
Et fredonnes tout bas de vieux airs inconnus;
Et quand descend le soir au manteau d'écarlate,
Tu poses doucement ton corps sur une natte,
Où tes rêves flottants sont pleins de colibris,
Et toujours, comme toi, gracieux et fleuris.
Pourquoi, l'heureuse enfant, veux-tu voir notre France,
Ce pays trop peuplé que fauche la souffrance,
Et, confiant ta vie aux bras forts des marins,
Faire de grands adieux à tes chers tamarins?
Toi, vêtue à moitié de mousselines frêles,
Frissonnante là-bas sous la neige et les grêles,
Comme tu pleurerais tes loisirs doux et francs
Si, le corset brutal emprisonnant tes flancs
Il te fallait glaner ton souper dans nos fanges
Et vendre le parfum de tes charmes étranges,
Oeil pensif, et suivant, dans nos sales brouillards,
Des cocotiers absents les fantômes épars!

Lady of the Coconut Trees

Woman from Malibar
let me build a hammock
across the expanse of your hips
and I will idle there;
lay down and feathers on your generous belly
and I will slumber deeply there.
Let me take each of your feet
to nurture and hold,
fledglings preparing to fly.
For safe-keeping
consign each of your treasure-filled hands
and I will teach them a new craft of loveplay.
Between the buttresses of your glorious thighs
I will scent the sweetness of pineapples
and the spice oils of your race.
Loosen your scarf one more time
and tamarind will infuse
my breathy kisses.
And no, I will not take you to stern France
where concrete and grey
will fade and reduce you
pavements and parks contain and drain you;
but rather my dark Malabaraise,
stay soft on your mat
in loose robes of muslin gather bounty,
bejewelled by tropical sunshine and rainfall,
the offerings of coconut trees
and solid men of the sea.

To A Woman from Malibar

Your feet are as fine-boned as your hands, and your generous hips /
would make even the most beautiful of white women envious. / The
thinking artist cherishes your sweet body; / your large velvet brown
eyes are darker than your skin. / In warm blue lands ordained by God
as your birthplace, / you faithfully light your master's pipe, / replenish
the jugs with fresh scented water, and chase pestering mosquitoes
from his bed. / When morning brings forth music from the plane trees,
/ you buy pineapples and bananas from the market. / All day long,
wandering barefoot and free, / you hum half-forgotten songs from
another time. / And when the scarlet mantle of nightfall descends, /
you gently place your body on your mat, / where your dreams, like
you, float with easy grace / among humming birds and flowers. / So
why, oh happy child, do you want to see this France of ours, / this
overcrowded place which sows only seeds of suffering? / And placing
your safety in the strong arms of your own seamen, / why bid farewell
to your treasured tamarind trees? / How you would mourn your
honest, simple life of ease, / as you shiver over there in snow and hail;
half dressed as you are and veiled only in delicate muslin. / And if,
your hips contained in cruel corsetry, / you had to scavenge for your
supper amongst the filth of our streets, / sell the exotic scent of your
charms, / your eyes would only fill with sorrow; / you would scan
our foggy, ugly landscapes just to catch a glimpse, maybe, / of the
scattered ghosts of your now far-off coconut trees.

Abel et Caïn

I
Race d'Abel, dors, bois et mange;
Dieu te sourit complaisamment.

Race de Caïn, dans la fange
Rampe et meurs misérablement.

Race d'Abel, ton sacrifice
Flatte le nez du Séraphin!

Race de Caïn, ton supplice
Aura-t-il jamais une fin?

Race d'Abel, vois tes semailles
Et ton bétail venir à bien;

Race de Caïn, tes entrailles
Hurlent la faim comme un vieux chien.

Race d'Abel, chauffe ton ventre
À ton foyer patriarcal;

Race de Caïn, dans ton antre
Tremble de froid, pauvre chacal!

Race d'Abel, aime et pullule!
Ton or fait aussi des petits.

Race de Caïn, coeur qui brûle,
Prends garde à ces grands appétits.

Seek the Righteous

Peter your great sin of denial is absolved
and Thomas's doubting no misdeed
for like Cleopatra's buried palaces of Alexandria
or Eden's Garden perhaps,
the gentle shepherd, Abel
clan chief of dreamers,
like a gazelle outrun in the chase
was struck down by a brother
deserted by the great Protector
and finally forgotten.

Since Adam's time
honourable blood has tinted the artist's canvas
and the songs of beggars
from ancient times
have oft even by chance pleaded quiet cause.
But there is no sandal-footed Jesus now,
scattering money lenders
like useless chaff;
for the wealthy predator holds our today,
like a shrinking lamb
in his crooked claw.
And tyrants stride like giants
casting whole nations into feckless seas
and babes, discarded puppets
lie face down on foreign sand

While the chattering salons of Paris
tittilate with aromatic tea
velvet and finery adorn the galleries
of our grand opera houses

Race d'Abel, tu croîs et broutes
Comme les punaises des bois!

Race de Caïn, sur les routes
Traîne ta famille aux abois.

II
Ah! race d'Abel, ta charogne
Engraissera le sol fumant!

Race de Caïn, ta besogne
N'est pas faite suffisamment;

Race d'Abel, voici ta honte:
Le fer est vaincu par l'épieu!

Race de Caïn, au ciel monte,
Et sur la terre jette Dieu!

women of the street, wine-blind ragpickers
and clochards of our bridges and backstreets
gather the excrement
of cravated plutocrats and the lisping oligarchs
of our cities.

Blessed is he who waits no more
Blessed is he who looks not to heaven
Blessed are the fallen angels who rise up
and found a city rich
with the forsaken just.

Abel and Cain

i

*Race of Abel, sleep, drink and eat; / Contentedly God smiles on you.
// Race of Cain, in the mud / Crawl miserably and die. // Race of
Abel, your sacrifice / Is pleasing to the Seraphim! // Race of Cain,
will your torture / Ever end? // Race of Abel, watch how the seeds
you have sown / And your cattle flourish and thrive. // Race of
Cain, your entrails scream out hunger, / like the whelping of an old
dog. // Race of Abel, warm your belly / at the warm hearth of your
ancestors. // Race of Cain, like the jackal, / Shiver with cold in your
lair. // Race of Abel, make love and multiply! / The precious gold
of your output will engender multitudes. // Race of Cain, with your
heart so on fire / And such great appetites, be vigilant. // Race of
Abel, you grow and feed freely / Like the bugs in the woods! // Race
of Cain, like a cornered animal / Drag your hapless family along
endless roads.*

ii

*Ah! Race of Abel, your carcass / will fertilise the humming earth. //
Race of Cain, your work / Is not completely done. // Race of Abel,
behold your shame: / Sabre overcome by the spear! // Race of Cain,
rise up to Heaven, / And cast God and his greatness to ground!*

L'Harmonie du Soir

Voici venir les temps où vibrant sur sa tige
Chaque fleur s'évapore ainsi qu'un encensoir;
Les sons et les parfums tournent dans l'air du soir;
Valse mélancolique et langoureux vertige!

Chaque fleur s'évapore ainsi qu'un encensoir;
Le violon frémit comme un coeur qu'on afflige;
Valse mélancolique et langoureux vertige!
Le ciel est triste et beau comme un grand reposoir.

Le violon frémit comme un coeur qu'on afflige,
Un coeur tendre, qui hait le néant vaste et noir!
Le ciel est triste et beau comme un grand reposoir;
Le soleil s'est noyé dans son sang qui se fige.

Un coeur tendre, qui hait le néant vaste et noir,
Du passé lumineux recueille tout vestige!
Le soleil s'est noyé dans son sang qui se fige...
Ton souvenir en moi luit comme un ostensoir!

Reverie

I pray you do not wake me
when the day is stilling
murmuring its leave-taking
and birds have paused their nesting
their feathers drifting like spring rain;
but rather let me rest awhile here
interred in chambered caves of settled night
warmed by precious oblivion;
where honey bees tumble soft on my brow
winds tease with shifts of reverie,
and I am suspended on silken threads of half words,
lulled by the cadence
of your breathing
and sweetened by the salt and grit of skin.

Harmony of Evening

*The hour approaches when flowers quiver on their stalks / their
fragments evaporate like incense from a burner; / sounds and scent
dance in the evening air; / oh melancholy waltz, oh slow heavy spin!
// Flowers quiver on their stalks, their fragments evaporate like
incense from a burner; / the violin throbs like a heart that is grief-
stricken; / oh melancholy waltz, oh slow heavy spin! / The sky is sad
and beautiful like a tabernacle of the great altar. // The violin throbs
like a heart that is grief-stricken; / a heart so tender, hates the vast
black void! / The sky is sad and beautiful like a tabernacle of the great
altar / The sun has cast itself into the depths of its own clotting blood.
// A heart so tender, hates the vast black void / it gathers the remains
of light from past times! / The sun has cast itself into the depths of its
own clotting blood / Every memory of you is a brilliant light in me,
shining out from a sacramental monstrance.*

Que diras-tu ce soir...

Que diras-tu ce soir, pauvre âme solitaire,
Que diras-tu, mon coeur, coeur autrefois flétri,
À la très belle, à la très bonne, à la très chère,
Dont le regard divin t'a soudain refleuri?

— Nous mettrons notre orgueil à chanter ses louanges:
Rien ne vaut la douceur de son autorité
Sa chair spirituelle a le parfum des Anges
Et son oeil nous revêt d'un habit de clarté.

Que ce soit dans la nuit et dans la solitude
Que ce soit dans la rue et dans la multitude
Son fantôme dans l'air danse comme un flambeau.

Parfois il parle et dit: «Je suis belle, et j'ordonne
Que pour l'amour de moi vous n'aimiez que le Beau;
Je suis l'Ange gardien, la Muse et la Madone.»

What will You Say Tonight?

*What will you say to her tonight, my poor lonely soul, / what will
you say tonight, my withered heart? / What will you say to the very
beautiful, most kind and dearest woman / whose gaze has suddenly
made me bloom anew. // We will harness our pride and together sing
her praises. / Nothing can equal the sweet joy of her dominion. / Her
flesh is a spirit redolent with the scent of angels. / Her eye cloaks us
in a fresh clarity. // Be it in the solitude of night / or in the multitudes
of day, / her ghost hovers and glides in the ether like a beacon. //
Sometimes it speaks and says "I am beautiful, and I command you /
for love of me, to love only Beauty; / I am your Guardian Angel, Muse
and Madonna.*

Cantique

It was a time my lady, of violets,
flowering your lips and your laughter,
flurries dropping full
 on time-warped bone
their scent pure on Cherubim's breath
and my perished heart;
a time of myths and musing
a *Vita Nuova*[3],
when swallows rose
arcing like rainbows
wings shivering to fan a vapid, laden sky
joy unlooked for
new-made skin.
Like the words of gods and giants
caught in history
your imprint lingers even now
but oh, I slept deeply then
on the smooth curve of a crescent moon
and at every morning time,
radiant
I circled the sun.

---

3   Apollonie Sabatier was a Muse and a source of inspiration for
    Baudelaire. Unlike his love poems to others with whom he had
    a relationship, his poems to her have a religious and respectful
    tone. The feel of them less overtly passionate and much more
    reflective and serene. In my response I have drawn on the poet's
    references in his work to Dante and Beatrice, Alighieri's own
    religious and spiritual guide in the final canticle and circles of
    Paradiso of the Divine Comedy. Vita Nuova is Dante's account
    of his first meeting and falling in love with Beatrice.

L'Invitation au Voyage

Mon enfant, ma soeur,
Songe à la douceur
D'aller là-bas vivre ensemble!
Aimer à loisir,
Aimer et mourir
Au pays qui te ressemble!
Les soleils mouillés
De ces ciels brouillés
Pour mon esprit ont les charmes
Si mystérieux
De tes traîtres yeux,
Brillant à travers leurs larmes.
Là, tout n'est qu'ordre et beauté,
Luxe, calme et volupté.

Des meubles luisants,
Polis par les ans,
Décoreraient notre chambre;
Les plus rares fleurs
Mêlant leurs odeurs
Aux vagues senteurs de l'ambre,
Les riches plafonds,
Les miroirs profonds,
La splendeur orientale,
Tout y parlerait
À l'âme en secret
Sa douce langue natale.
Là, tout n'est qu'ordre et beauté,
Luxe, calme et volupté.

Vois sur ces canaux

In Candlelight

Oh let me loosen my corsets and let fall my chaste cloths
on gentle willow;
as you gaze,
let me unclasp my hair at last
and sprinkle amber stones and yellow diamonds
over pillows of pale satin,
where you now lie
adorned in the willing scent and crescent fullness of me;
attired only in silken coverlets from Samarkand
we are framed by marquetry and rich mahogany
and deep within the mirrored walls of our bedchamber
buried in teeming wells of love
the tang of bitter oranges and cinnamon
on our unschooled lips,
let us abandon fruitless shame
and in our reckless search
discover new purpose,
a new tongue for pleasure without end
and a tireless leavening
each of the other.
The boats will slip by our windows
and like the hours on a clock
we will neither need nor heed their steady passing,
guided only by the gathering shades of ardour
flamed by a thousand and one candles.

Dormir ces vaisseaux
Dont l'humeur est vagabonde;
C'est pour assouvir
Ton moindre désir
Qu'ils viennent du bout du monde.
— Les soleils couchants
Revêtent les champs,
Les canaux, la ville entière,
D'hyacinthe et d'or;
Le monde s'endort
Dans une chaude lumière.
Là, tout n'est qu'ordre et beauté,
Luxe, calme et volupté.

An Invitation to Journey

My child and sister, / think of hours of bliss, / imagine a journey,
and living together somewhere / With time to love, / time to love and
to die, / in a land that is not unlike you! / Moist suns and skies of
soft mist / to my mind, have the same mystery and charm / as your
treacherous eyes shining through your tears. // In a place of harmony
and beauty let us luxuriate in pleasure. // Polished mahogany /
seasoned by years / would furnish our bedchamber; / scents from the
rarest of flowers / mingle with the faint waft of amber, sumptuous
ceilings / and cavernous mirrors, / all the splendours of the East,
whisper words / only the soul can understand. // In a place of
harmony and beauty let us luxuriate in pleasure. // See how soundly
/ sail boats, stilled from wandering, / now slumber in these canals;
/ they are come from all the ends of the earth / to satisfy your every
whim. / Watch the setting suns / cloak the fields, / the canals, and
the entire town / in indigo and gold; / and robed in a warm light / the
world finally drifts into sleep. // In a place of harmony and beauty /
let us luxuriate in pleasure.

Les Bijoux

La très chère était nue, et, connaissant mon coeur,
Elle n'avait gardé que ses bijoux sonores,
Dont le riche attirail lui donnait l'air vainqueur
Qu'ont dans leurs jours heureux les esclaves des Mores.

Quand il jette en dansant son bruit vif et moqueur,
Ce monde rayonnant de métal et de pierre
Me ravit en extase, et j'aime à la fureur
Les choses où le son se mêle à la lumière.

Elle était donc couchée et se laissait aimer,
Et du haut du divan elle souriait d'aise
À mon amour profond et doux comme la mer,
Qui vers elle montait comme vers sa falaise.

Les yeux fixés sur moi, comme un tigre dompté,
D'un air vague et rêveur elle essayait des poses,
Et la candeur unie à la lubricité
Donnait un charme neuf à ses métamorphoses;

Et son bras et sa jambe, et sa cuisse et ses reins,
Polis comme de l'huile, onduleux comme un cygne,
Passaient devant mes yeux clairvoyants et sereins;
Et son ventre et ses seins, ces grappes de ma vigne,

S'avançaient, plus câlins que les Anges du mal,
Pour troubler le repos où mon âme était mise,
Et pour la déranger du rocher de cristal
Où, calme et solitaire, elle s'était assise.

How Pale the Daylight

Come Madame, come
and dismiss pale daylight I pray you
for we have no use for it
but rather,
rough and unclothed, adorned only in frippery,
loosen your brass anklets as you weave and shift,
by the light of lanterns
throw off your
silver clasps and fastenings
let each of your footsteps
cast a sunbeam as you dance
and your encrusted hands craft
silvered fantasy on close walls;
while your every gesture gathers me in,
like a giant oak advance on me my love
shower me with the breath of blown branches
and the sweet dews of licence;
and murmuring loose words of loveplay
eager, bid me travel the oiled wood and grain
of your lush, undulating frame
my only music the low hum of your pleasure
and the joy of manacles.

Je croyais voir unis par un nouveau dessin
Les hanches de l'Antiope au buste d'un imberbe,
Tant sa taille faisait ressortir son bassin.
Sur ce teint fauve et brun, le fard était superbe!

— Et la lampe s'étant résignée à mourir,
Comme le foyer seul illuminait la chambre
Chaque fois qu'il poussait un flamboyant soupir,
Il inondait de sang cette peau couleur d'ambre!

The Jewels

My treasure was naked, and knowing my deepest wish, / she wore only jewellery; the jingle-jangle / of her dazzling, rich adornment / giving her a conquering air / like a sated Moorish concubine.' // This resplendent, teasing interplay / of ringing metal and glittering gems, / thrills me to the point of ecstasy / and I have a passion for that fusion of sound and light. // Stretched out on a couch she let me love her, / she smiled down languidly / at my intense, tender lovemaking which like a gathering wave, / rose up towards her like the sea towards the cliff face. // She watched me closely and like a tamed tigress / she dreamily posed this way and that, / her every easy, relaxed posture, / her raw sensuality and hunger / gracing each new presentation with charm. // Her arms, her legs, her thighs and her back like oiled wood, / undulating and swan-like passed before my eyes, / and watchful, I calmly followed her every move. / Her belly and her breasts, clusters of fruit to my vine, // Advancing towards me, were more alluring than the Angels of darkness, / disturbing my serenity and dislodging my soul / from the crystal rock / where it had settled, alone and still. // So deep was the thrusting of her loins that it seemed as if by some new design, / Antiope's hips had been joined to the bust of a boy. / How superbly the maquillage of her eyes and mouth / mingled with the bronze and mellow hues of her skin. // And in the dying light of the lamp / the room was lit by fire alone, which with every flaming sigh / bathed her amber skin in blood.

Le Crépuscule du soir

Voici le soir charmant, ami du criminel;
Il vient comme un complice, à pas de loup; le ciel
Se ferme lentement comme une grande alcôve,
Et l'homme impatient se change en bête fauve.

Ô soir, aimable soir, désiré par celui
Dont les bras, sans mentir, peuvent dire: Aujourd'hui
Nous avons travaillé! — C'est le soir qui soulage
Les esprits que dévore une douleur sauvage,
Le savant obstiné dont le front s'alourdit,
Et l'ouvrier courbé qui regagne son lit.
Cependant des démons malsains dans l'atmosphère
S'éveillent lourdement, comme des gens d'affaire,
Et cognent en volant les volets et l'auvent.
À travers les lueurs que tourmente le vent
La Prostitution s'allume dans les rues;
Comme une fourmilière elle ouvre ses issues;
Partout elle se fraye un occulte chemin,
Ainsi que l'ennemi qui tente un coup de main;
Elle remue au sein de la cité de fange
Comme un ver qui dérobe à l'Homme ce qu'il mange.
On entend çà et là les cuisines siffler,
Les théâtres glapir, les orchestres ronfler;
Les tables d'hôte, dont le jeu fait les délices,
S'emplissent de catins et d'escrocs, leurs complices,
Et les voleurs, qui n'ont ni trêve ni merci,
Vont bientôt commencer leur travail, eux aussi,
Et forcer doucement les portes et les caisses
Pour vivre quelques jours et vêtir leurs maîtresses.

Recueille-toi, mon âme, en ce grave moment,

A Welcome Dusk

At the lighting of the lamps
bid me stir then
to hail a faint dusk
nightfall bristling in its shadow
nature's seedlings turned sluggish and shy
grasses hushed.

Let me bathe
in waters slowing silver
grasp a city's gemstones brilliant in the greying air
while palaces and churches
fade into the gathering void.

Treading stark flagstones
emptied of the day's light,
in other company
I will dance a solemn sarabande;
in caverns redolent with wine
and sweet decay,
greet those worthy guardians
and beacons of my nights.

Et ferme ton oreille à ce rugissement.
C'est l'heure où les douleurs des malades s'aigrissent!
La sombre Nuit les prend à la gorge; ils finissent
Leur destinée et vont vers le gouffre commun;
L'hôpital se remplit de leurs soupirs. — Plus d'un
Ne viendra plus chercher la soupe parfumée,
Au coin du feu, le soir, auprès d'une âme aimée.

Encore la plupart n'ont-ils jamais connu
La douceur du foyer et n'ont jamais vécu!

Dusk

*Sweet evening arrives like an accomplice; / the criminal's friend
steals in like a wolf; / the sky closes over like a great alcove / and the
impatient man turns into a wild and predatory animal. // Oh gentle
evening, longed for by men / whose arms, speak no lie, when they
say: Today / we have laboured! Evening soothes / a soul ravaged by
profound grief, / the heavy brow of the stubborn scholar / and the
back-bent worker trudging home to bed. / Meanwhile unholy demons
slowly come forth from the ether / and set about their business, /
bumping into shutters and awnings, / in the light of lanterns flickering
in the wind. / Prostitution lights up the streets. / She is an anthill, her
every channel and orifice wide open, / she makes her louche way like
an enemy set to strike; / she wades through the city's mud and detritus
/ like a worm gulping the food of hungry men. / Whistling kitchens
burst into sound, / theatres screech their presence, orchestras scrape
and wheeze; / gaming tables of pleasure and chance / fill with harlots
and gangsters and their cronies, / and thieves who never stop nor
have any mercy, / will soon begin their own work, / gently bursting
door locks and safes / to fund a few days of luxury or new clothes
for a mistress. / Hold back, my soul, at this perilous time, / shut your
ears to this cacophony. / Now is the hour when the afflicted suffer
most; sombre night takes them by the throat; their journeying over,
/ darkness leads them to the common pit; / hospitals echo with their
painful sighing. Never more / will they sit with a loved one / warmed
by a fireside and the aroma of soup. // Most of them have never
known / the sweetness of a hearth nor have they ever fully tasted life.*

Le Flacon

Il est de forts parfums pour qui toute matière
Est poreuse. On dirait qu'ils pénètrent le verre.
En ouvrant un coffret venu de l'Orient
Dont la serrure grince et rechigne en criant,

Ou dans une maison déserte quelque armoire
Pleine de l'âcre odeur des temps, poudreuse et noire,
Parfois on trouve un vieux flacon qui se souvient,
D'où jaillit toute vive une âme qui revient.

Mille pensers dormaient, chrysalides funèbres,
Frémissant doucement dans les lourdes ténèbres,
Qui dégagent leur aile et prennent leur essor,
Teintés d'azur, glacés de rose, lamés d'or.

Voilà le souvenir enivrant qui voltige
Dans l'air troublé; les yeux se ferment; le Vertige
Saisit l'âme vaincue et la pousse à deux mains
Vers un gouffre obscurci de miasmes humains;

Il la terrasse au bord d'un gouffre séculaire,
Où, Lazare odorant déchirant son suaire,
Se meut dans son réveil le cadavre spectral
D'un vieil amour ranci, charmant et sépulcral.

Ainsi, quand je serai perdu dans la mémoire
Des hommes, dans le coin d'une sinistre armoire
Quand on m'aura jeté, vieux flacon désolé,
Décrépit, poudreux, sale, abject, visqueux, fêlé,

Je serai ton cercueil, aimable pestilence!

Epilogue

The waft of you blows through me still
the warm, sweet ooze of you
edging my skin, lapping hollowed bone,
oft commands my heartbeat
takes me unaware;
and when I stand distracted in a city street
I am suddenly felled
by the gleaming memory of mica
your steady gaze from within a crowd;
from a tall cathedral or castle turret
I am too frequently
transfixed by each feature of your absent face
on a multitude of faces below me;
and by the river's sparkle
caught on the curve and shimmer of your unforgotten lips
by wings of butterflies
I am stilled.
I still carry the music of you
trumpeting and teasing
or simply joyous
on my breath,
and the thunder and radiance of you
the hurricanes and droughts
of your changing countenance
like the squalls of springtime
still slow my footstep
loosen my hold.

Madonna shall I ever call you by a lesser name?

Le témoin de ta force et de ta virulence,
Cher poison préparé par les anges! liqueur
Qui me ronge, ô la vie et la mort de mon coeur!

The Perfume Bottle

There are some perfumes so strong / that they make any material porous. They even seem to penetrate glass. / If you open a casket from the East, / the locks grating, creaking and squealing, // Or a dark, dusty wardrobe in a derelict house / full of acrid smells of the past, / often you will find a memory-filled perfume bottle / from whence a forgotten soul will spring forth and return to the present. // A thousand sombre thoughts / gently quivering in the impenetrable dark will emerge from their chrysalis, / spread their wings and fly, / tinted blue, glazed in pink, or burnished with gold. // This dizzying memory once materialised revolves constantly. / If you close your eyes, in the troubling air, / vertigo will take hold of your vanquished soul and with both hands / thrust it towards the pit that lurks beneath man's foul reek. // Lay it down on the rim of an ancient pit / where evil smelling Lazarus rends his burial cloths asunder; / and his spectral corpse, like an old love affair and the stink of age, / in its reawakening, is transformed, into charming solemnity. // Likewise when I am gone from the memory of humankind, / in the corner of a sinister wardrobe / where they will have tossed me, like a sad old perfume bottle, / decrepit, dusty, dirtied, vile, slimy, cracked, // I will be your winding cloth. Such a pleasurable plague! / I will be witness to your strength and your potency. / Sweet poison made by angels! Oh liquor that never ceases to tempt me. / Oh you, both life and death of my heart.

Selected Bibliography

Baudelaire as a Love Poet and Other Essays; Hyslop, Lois Boe; 1969

Baudelaire in Chains: Portrait of the Artist as a Drug Addict; Hilton, Frank; 2004

Baudelaire's World; Lloyd, Rosemary; 2002

Cambridge Companion to Baudelaire; Loyd, Rosemary; 2005

Baudelaire Les Fleurs du Mal; ed. Pichois, Claude; 1996

Baudelaire; Richardson, Joanna; 1994

Charles Baudelaire: A Life in Writing; Jackson in Lloyd; 2005

Baudelaire's Poetic Journey; Wright, Barbara, in Lloyd; 2005

Baudelaire and Feminine Singularity; Chatterjee; 2005

How the French Think; Hazareesingh; 2015